LET THE UNIVERSE LEAD YOU!

LET THE UNIVERSE LEAD YOU!

How To Follow The Path To Your Manifestations

RICHARD DOTTS

© Richard Dotts 2015
1st Edition
ISBN-13: 9781522875048
ISBN-10 1522875042
Questions / comments? The author can be contacted at RichardDotts@gmail.com

Table of Contents

Chapter One	Let the Universe Lead You!	1
Chapter Two	You Can Both Lead and Follow at the Same Time	9
Chapter Three	The Universe Knows All Ways... So Let It!	17
Chapter Four	The Art of Reverse Manifestations	27
Chapter Five	The Pure Essence of Joy in Our Final Manifestations	36
Chapter Six	Higher and Higher, Better and Better	46
Chapter Seven	The Universe Always Nudges You in the Right Direction	54
Chapter Eight	You Always Get the Vibrational Essence of What You Ask For	63
Chapter Nine	Practical Ways to Let the Universe Lead You	72
Chapter Ten	The Reverse Manifestations Process	79

Chapter One
Let The Universe Lead You!

I was driving a friend home the other night when I felt inspired to offer some strange but soothing words to him. Words he would not have expected to hear from me. Normally I would not speak about certain subjects except through these books, but I suddenly felt inspired that evening on the quiet drive back. Cruising along the freeway, I felt the Universe nudging me along, urging me to get those words out of my mouth. I could not hold on to them any longer.

I have learned many times that when the time is right for you to hear a message, the Universe will send messengers into your life to bring you *exactly* what you need to know. You will be given the missing piece you need at that moment in time, but rarely a moment sooner. If you need guidance, the next step will be shown to you. If you need a nudge that you are moving in the right direction, a sign will be given to you as well. Divine guidance always comes along at the right place and at the right time although such guidance may take many forms—a book title (my favorite), a movie title, song lyrics, offhand remarks, or even sudden blocks of thoughts and emotions that come to you. Sometimes, you may even feel a clear, inexplicable impulse to go *do* something.

And so that evening, I became the messenger.

I noticed this friend of mine struggling quite a bit lately. He was doing well on the outside by most standards, but I could also tell that he was worn out and weary on the inside. He was trying to do so many different things at once, taking the paths and chasing the opportunities that came his way.

His way of operating in the world is all too familiar because I lived my life in exactly the same manner just a few short years ago. Back then, I always worried about whether I could "make it" in the world and whether I would eventually achieve the level of wealth and success I hoped for. Uncertainty, fear, and doubt swirled endlessly in my mind as I frequently pondered what I should do next to "chase my dreams." Since success seemed so uncertain, I saw the need to take as much action as possible to improve my chances in life. Sounds familiar?

Little did I know that this was a totally backward way of living. Instead of making me happier and more assured, I became more stressed with each step I took. Hearing about the success of others discouraged me and made me resentful. I wondered why I was still going nowhere despite taking massive action. I read and devoured one self-help book after another, amassing a library of thousands of books and courses by the time I turned 21. Yet I felt as if there was still a void within me!

I tried seeking outside help by consulting with psychics and experts in their various fields. I was determined to get the knowledge I needed not only from this world but from "other" worlds as well. How foolish I was! Each of them offered their own well-meaning advice, but as I tried to mold myself into their definitions of success by following their way, I felt increasingly estranged from my own true self. I was moving further and further away from my own inner calling. There was very little joy in my life as I was pulled into these different directions by the so-called experts.

As I look back, I finally understand what I was looking for all those years. I thought I was looking for the path to success or even the secret to success, but I wasn't. I was searching for something far more basic and fundamental than that. I was looking for that sense of *certainty*. I was looking for a way to eliminate all the uncertainties in my life, for the Universe to finally look at me in the eye and say, "Look, I have taken all the uncertainties out of your life. Now you can be assured that whatever you do from now on will be just right for you and will not put you in harm's way. You will not fail." Those were the words I had been yearning to hear from the Universe.

As I looked into my friend's eyes earlier that evening, I saw that he was also looking everywhere for that sense of *certainty*. He was looking for a sure path that would bring him the success and riches he envisioned in life so that he could feel safe and secure forever. With that, I felt my lips parting as these words came out of my mouth:

"Do you know the one realization I wish I had when I was in your position many years ago?"

"Erm…no. What is it?" he asked, hanging on to my every word.

"If there is anything I learned from my years of struggle, it is this: *Stop trying so hard.* You need to stop trying so hard and let the Universe lead you on where to go next."

While I continued glancing at the road ahead, I could see him fidgeting in his seat from the corner of my eye, visibly surprised by my words. I could tell that he had not expected this from me, someone whom he had always seen as hardworking. Yet I wanted to let him know that there exists an *inner* path to success.

"From the outside, I probably achieve 10 times more than what I used to in the past. But on the inside, it does not feel as if I am working any harder. Truth be told, I am working much less than before. I put in less hours than before but get more done. That's because I am letting the Universe guide me now. I look for alignment on the inside before taking any physical action on the outside," I continued.

"Do you mean to think more about what I want on the inside?" he asked.

"No, that's not what I mean. You already know what you want. What I'm saying is to stop figuring out *how* you will get it. Leave that part to the Universe who will show it to you when the time is right. Do not take action just for the sake of taking action so as to try and 'make something happen.' Instead, be still and listen to what is happening on the inside. Take action only when you feel inspired."

I don't know whether he eventually got my message, but I'm sure glad to have planted the seed in him. The seed of possibilities will germinate when the conditions are right. Then I realized that this message is so important that it should probably be turned into a book. This message, if understood and applied correctly in one's life, will save you from years of needless struggle, agony, and self-criticism. This is the piece of the puzzle that, if understood, catapults and places you immediately onto the fast track of success.

I realize today that I could have taken the magic elevator through life and cut through all the self-imposed limitations or worries had I achieved this understanding sooner. How thankful I am to know that the Universe we live in is a benevolent one and that nothing can possibly go wrong for us even if we *tried!* Nothing that we do can possibly put us in harm's way if we are in tune with our own inner guidance. Ironically, it is only when we act out of alignment with our own inner voice that we are led off the path into seemingly "dangerous" situations.

If there is anything I can tell my former self today, it would be this: *All is well.* You are just where you need to be. You are at the right place at the right time.

As I told my friend later on in the conversation, "Never look at where you are and resent yourself for not doing/being more. Never look at the success or achievements of others and blame yourself for not living up to the same standards. Everyone has different paths in life and is at different stages of their journey. We are all doing the best we can, given what we know. Therefore, there is nothing that can ever come out of comparing yourself with others. All comparison merely perpetuates the false belief that we should be somewhere else other than where we are in the moment."

Understand that no matter where you are in life right now, your current circumstances did not come about by chance. Instead (and broadly speaking), they are the cumulative effects of your long-held thoughts, actions, feelings, and beliefs. Your thoughts and feelings make up your inner state. In other words, your outer reality today is predicated by your inner world.

The reason why so many people look so hard for that sense of certainty in their lives is because they wrongly believe their world to be based on luck or chance. Since they are not fully aware of the *direct* linkage between their inner thoughts and outer reality, they perceive events in their outer world to happen *by chance*. But as you slowly cultivate a clearer view of your inner state, you'll be able to attribute outer events exactly to their inner causes, every single time. This also means that by making a shift on the inside, you can cause circumstances to change on the outside without your physical intervention.

With this realization, one no longer lives their life in an outer-directed manner. An outer-directed way of life means one is always searching for and seeking the "right" path that can produce results in the fastest way. This way of life hinges heavily on our own discipline, intellect, and willpower while denying that a higher power has always existed to support us in our endeavors. An outer-directed life means that our actions make up for our inner doubts and insecurities. We end up doing things we shouldn't and saying things we shouldn't just to cover up that sense of smallness or weakness inside.

When you finally accept that you are just all right wherever you are, you understand (somewhat counterintuitively) that you are *always* at the best place you can possibly be. That's why Abraham-Hicks have repeatedly said, "You are where you are!" Indeed, I am where I am! This is not just a way of making ourselves *feel* better; it is also a reflection of the highest truth. Everyone is at the best place they can possibly be in life given their current level of consciousness. We are always living up to the fullness of our current potential, given everything we already know and do. If we *could* be somewhere else, we would already be there. Therefore, don't believe in the mistaken premise that you could be there "faster" if there is some shortcut or "secret" action that you should have taken. This self-critical way of thinking must first be corrected for much-desired results to occur in one's life. Let all the blame, discouragement, and resentment end here now.

When I first heard Abraham-Hicks teach that "I am (just right) where I am" in life, I had a very difficult time accepting their logic. Some of you may undoubtedly feel the same way. But stick with me as we progress through this book and I'll show you why results will happen on the outside once you overcome your inner hurdle of self-imposed expectations. I'll show you why the art of manifestations has never been about *making* things happen but all about *letting* things happen. As you shift your inner attitude from one of looking for certainty in an uncertain world to *knowing* that all is well in every moment of your life, you step into the best version of yourself. As you go from trying to influence things to *letting* things happen and being in the flow, you unleash the cooperative forces of the Universe. The entire Universe conspires on your behalf!

This is not just a fantasy. It is a reality that you can live once you decide to *let the Universe lead you!*

Chapter Two
You Can Both Lead And Follow At The Same Time

There is a certain stigma in our culture attached to being a follower. All of us want to become leaders in our respective fields, at our workplaces and in our careers. All of us want to, in the words of a popular self-help program, "lead the field." Hardly anyone wants to be a follower. There is a negative connotation attached to the notion of being led, as it suggests that we are weak or that we are incapable in some way.

But that's not what letting the Universe lead you is about. Letting the Universe lead you is *not* about becoming a passive follower and giving up your power. It's not about becoming inactive or weak and letting others decide for you, although that's how these teachings have often been misunderstood. It's not about surrendering or giving up either. We are not teaching a course in surrendering or giving up your good.

Contrary to all that, letting the Universe lead you is about reclaiming your power as a true creator. It's about recognizing that you've always had these creative abilities within yourself to make anything happen, and that you are now finally willing to let the Universe be on your side. For far too long and especially in this modern age, mankind has been refusing the help of any higher or spiritual power, preferring to depend on his own superior intellect or his technologically advanced tools. And yet for all the modern advancements and breakthroughs our civilization has made, there remains problems at every level of society that have not been solved. Fundamental problems about how our societies and governments are organized. Problems with hunger and with poverty in various parts of the world. Why is it that we are unable to solve these various problems despite our superior human intellect?

Maybe the answer we are looking for is far simpler than anything we have ever imagined: We have been using the wrong tools and looking in the wrong places. We have been looking *outside* of ourselves for answers whereas they have always resided *within* ourselves. Our sophisticated scientific equipment and tools help us to peer 10 to 15 billion light-years away, yet the answers we seek have not been found there. Perhaps it is time to seriously embrace and consider what the spiritual masters have reaffirmed throughout the ages: that the answers are *within ourselves.*

Let's think about this from an individual perspective for a moment. Forget about all the major "problems" and "issues" plaguing the world. Forget about poverty, illnesses, pollution, governments, unrest. Focus just on your own life. Take a good look at your own life and what has unfolded so far. Would you say that the best answers to some of the biggest questions you asked have come from within? Would you say that your intuition and gut feeling have proven to be right fairly often, even though your logical mind has told you otherwise? And would you also say that some of the best things in your life happened to you because you followed your intuition and inner calling?

I've had this conversation literally hundreds of times with people from all over the world, from diverse backgrounds and with different levels of spiritual understanding. Each of them has personally told me the following: One, that their gut feeling about a situation has often turned out to be remarkably accurate, even though their logical mind was fighting it all the way. Two, that some of the best opportunities happened as a result of following their intuition and inner calling. Till today, I've never met a single person who said, "I followed my inner calling and it led me to a bad place." Not a single person has told me so. Doesn't that tell us something already about the power of our inner wisdom?

I'm willing to wager that no matter where you are in the world, what I've said rings true to you to a certain extent. You may still not trust in your intuition and inner nudges completely, but I think you will agree that it has helped you at least once or twice in life. Even the old skeptical (and extremely scientific) me can pinpoint several instances in my life where I was just led to take a particular action at exactly the right moment. Had I taken the action a moment sooner or later, the opportunity would have been lost forever. Such things simply cannot be fully explained using plain scientific logic, as they go beyond the spheres of what our scientific instruments can accurate perceive and measure.

So there is no need to look far and out into the galaxies for living proof that this stuff works. Look within yourself. You'll find at least one or two instances there. Why not build upon these successes and turn them into a regular way of life? Why not find out how those nudges came about in the first place and start tapping into your inner creative insights more often? When I raise this suggestion, people often say, "Oh, but those instances were just pure coincidences. I don't get them all the time."

Do you see what just happened here? We place so much faith and trust in our scientific models and equipment that we dismiss any of these happenings as mere luck, chance, or coincidences! And yet when you truly think about the *chances* of something like that happening, you would have to admit that the statistical chances are truly minuscule. Case in point: After years of not having any financial breakthrough, someone decides to try a clearing process that drops a few long-held negative beliefs about money. Soon after that, the phone starts ringing out of the blue and an old client offers you a new engagement. Would that be pure coincidence, or would it be the direct result of having done the inner work?

Years of doing the inner work has convinced me that it is the latter. The more you do the inner work and cultivate your inner states, the greater clarity and power you'll reclaim. You will realize that events and circumstances in your life are never just mere coincidences. Instead, everything has been orchestrated *by* the Universe *on* your behalf, as a direct response to the thoughts, feelings, and intentions that you hold or once held. Similarly, anything unwanted in your life is also the result of recurring thought patterns of beliefs, many of which may be unconscious to you right now. As you become more aware of whatever is happening in your inner state on a moment-by-moment basis, you'll regain so much clarity that you'll be able to stop self-sabotaging behaviors and events in their tracks. You'll no longer get in your own way.

When someone asks me for "proof" that this works, I never tell them to look far. The answer does not lie in looking outside of ourselves. Instead, I've always asked the same few questions: Have miracles happened to you in life? If so, what were the circumstances and conditions that caused those miracles to happen? Did you have to do anything for those miracles to happen? When we look back at our own lives, we often do not have to look far to find miracles that have taken place. Miracles happen to all of us on a regular basis. If we'll open our eyes to them, we will find them. But one must be careful not to be overly cynical or skeptical and dismiss everything as coincidence.

Just a few weeks ago I was flying and had the intention of upgrading my plane ticket at a good price. The airlines are always strict about upgrading only one class at a time, which means that one can never jump, let's say, from economy to first class while skipping business class in between. Imagine my surprise when the counter staff did so for me with no questions asked. I had literally bent the rules in front of my own eyes! I just believed it could be done and asked for it. Now one may say that this was a fluke, or that the lady was just being kind… But isn't the lady being kind *also* a miracle of some sort? I still think it is so absolutely beautiful to meet beautiful people who are willing to assist me at every turn. Speaking of which, I was desperately trying to locate some information using my smartphone at the airports when a ground attendant literally stopped me and asked, "Is there something you may need help with?" That was certainly a first that happened to me. I knew that there were counters that one could approach to ask for help, but I was never *stopped* in my tracks and *asked* if I needed help! Another miracle there to help you along your day.

When you open yourself up to receiving help, you'll be surprised at all kinds of channels and resources that suddenly open up to you. I am talking about this at a spiritual level. There is a tendency for us to be overly skeptical and guarded, especially in this day and age. We tend not to trust others so much, preferring to rely on our own intellect and judgment to sieve through all the information that is presented to us. While doing all of that, let's not forget that higher powers and higher channels are always available to us. I'll expand on these in the chapters that follow, but I would like to remind you at this juncture not to dismiss anything that comes into your life. Every piece is here (or has been sent here) for a reason. If you dismiss everything that happens as a mere coincidence without examining the deeper significance of things, you'll be missing out on many beautiful moments of life.

Be open and receptive to words of advice and gestures that may be extended to you as you go about your daily activities. Become receptive to accepting help. For one, learning to say "yes" more often to help is a good start as it changes our mindset about being led. As you'll realize in the next few chapters, being led is not about becoming passive and inactive. It's not about sitting there and doing nothing. Far from that. It is all about becoming proactive and taking action. But it's action taken *on the inside.* Learn how to take action to change what happens *on the inside.* When you do so, you make room for things to transform spontaneously on the outside.

Many years ago, when I first learned about opening myself up to Universal guidance, I ended up becoming unintentionally stuck in one of the worst ruts of my life! I had read into this piece of advice too literally and just sat there all day, not thinking or doing anything. I was literally waiting for the Universe to tell me what to do, what I should create, or what opportunities I should go for. But that's not how the Universe works! Inaction will only attract more inaction, just as action can only attract more action. Therefore, opening up yourself to Universal guidance is not about sitting there and letting the Universe *tell* you what to do next. It's not about being spoon-fed and led like a flock. Instead, it is about *deciding very clearly what you want* and then opening yourself up to receiving it in the fastest, most direct and harmonious way. Since our limited physical senses do not allow us to perceive all possible ways at once, we leave that part up to the Universe. We let the miraculous Universe lead and nudge us into what is the best way for us. The leading and the guidance occurs *after* we have decided on what we wanted and communicated it clearly to the Universe…*but not a moment sooner.* Let's take a look at how you can do so right now, starting today…

Chapter Three
The Universe Knows All Ways...So Let It!

The infinite Universe knows all things. It knows what you want and how to deliver it to you in the fastest way possible. In fact, not only does it know what *you* want, it also knows the exact preferences of billions of other individuals on this planet. The Universe is constantly picking up on all these impulses, coordinating them and then making things happen in the best way possible for everyone. Think of the Universe as a giant dealmaker, always trying to match the needs and preferences of one person with another's. This process happens round-the-clock with such regularity and consistency that we often take it for granted. We see it just as the natural movement and flow of life, forgetting that a grand orchestration is in fact happening every moment.

I have often taught that the Universe knows *exactly* what you want the moment you hold an intention. Therefore, there is no need to worry about whether the Universe has picked up on your intentions and desires clearly. The Universe always gets it right the first time! What most people do not also realize is that the moment you hold an intention, the Universe simultaneously *knows* the best way to make it happen for you.

Because it has such a macro view of the entire situation, the Universe is able to immediately identify ways in which your desired good can be delivered to you. If you understand this Universal principle, you'll never fret over *how* something is going to come to you. No physical limitations will ever matter to you again. You just know that in the moment you ask, it is done!

Abraham-Hicks have taught that in any moment, there are no less than seven "very real" possibilities and ways through which a particular manifestation can happen for you. Can you imagine that? No matter what you ask for, there are at least seven *direct* ways in which the Universe can make it happen in your life *right now*...and that's just the beginning! If you consider all the indirect ways through which something can come to you, then the possibilities are truly endless. There are infinite ways through which your manifestations can happen for you, far more than what each of us can physically perceive in the moment.

If that's the case, why is it that our manifestations sometimes seem so far away from us? Why do we not always get the things we ask for? I have addressed this several times in my previous books but it is worth repeating here. We often trip ourselves up because of our self-imposed feelings of worry, discouragement, and fear. We often worry endlessly over whether we can get what we ask for and impose unnecessary time limits on our manifestations.

Since the Universe always picks up on our feelings and not on our physical words/preferences, all our negative feelings become an *intention* of their own as well. In other words, when you think about what you want and then also think many other worrisome thoughts associated with that intention... your original intention becomes contradictory and diluted. You'll be asking hard for what you want on one hand and contradicting it with negative thoughts of fears and worries on the other. Those fearful and worrisome thoughts are intentions in and of themselves as well. They are intentions for more situations to feel fearful or worried about, although that is certainly not what you are asking for on a conscious level. The result is no physical manifestations.

The simple key to manifestations is this: If you are able to completely remove all negative thoughts related to your manifestations, then they have to happen very quickly. In other words, when you think about what you want, think about it purely with absolutely no contradictions in your vibrations. Once you get to that place, then the physical manifestations have to happen extremely quickly...they are the next logical step! However, if you are unable to think about your intentions without feeling some discord or worry about whether/how/when you'll get them...then these negative feelings are the causes of your delay. Eliminate them and your manifestations happen quickly.

This is perhaps the most important lesson to learn no matter what it is you are trying to manifest in life. Take time to practice training your own vibrations and your own inner state. Become acutely aware of how you feel in each moment on the inside. More importantly, drop whatever feelings that are not in harmony with your highest intentions and desires. This means dropping your feelings of worry, fear, discouragement, blame, guilt, and resentment from your inner state. Be free of them and everything good will be added unto you.

Now what I have just described are the theoretical aspects of manifestations. But how do we put all of that into practice? Despite their best efforts, some people cannot help but feel discouraged or worried about how their manifestations will come to them. Some people cannot help but worry over how they will meet that tight deadline, or how they will receive a particular sum of money to take care of that financial need. If this sounds like you, then I have some good news for you. I have simplified it down to a simple series of steps and broader principles. Follow them and you'll automatically be in harmony with these Universal Laws.

Here's an example. Let's suppose that you have asked for something very hard and put all these techniques into practice. You have tried to think about your desires purely and eliminated most of the negative vibrations from your inner state. But still, nothing is happening (or it seems like so).

As an example, let's assume that you are trying to manifest a new car but have no idea how it is going to come to you. The most obvious route to you would be to use whatever money you have to buy the car from the dealer outright. But there is one problem: You do not have sufficient funds to make the purchase at the moment. And so you start thinking about various ways and means through which you can close the shortfall within a certain period of time. "How can I earn an extra $20,000 in the next three months so I can afford the car?" is a logical question that may run through your mind. "Perhaps I can ask the bank for a loan or launch a new product that will generate cash for me fast."

Let's take a look at a few manifestation pitfalls we have fallen into without even realizing it. First, by deciding that we will purchase the car outright and then figuring out how to get the money, we have fallen into the trap of insisting that the final manifestation happens for us *in a certain way*. "I will use my own money to purchase this car by figuring out how to make up the shortfall" is the message that we are sending to the Universe. Now that is usually not a bad thing, for you *can* certainly ask for something and also be clear about the path through which it comes to you. However, it is often the second part that trips people up. When we decide that something is going to come to us through a particular way, we usually fret over how to make it happen. This is a pervasive trap that most of us fall into all the time without even realizing it.

By worrying over how we will generate $20,000 in three weeks to purchase the car, we are throwing ourselves vibrationally off-balance with regards to our original intention. Imposing a deadline just makes those feelings worse. Instead of thinking about what we want purely, we have now thrown intense feelings of worry and desperation into the mix. Therefore, each time we think about the car, we are actually thinking about *how* to make that sum of money so we can afford it.

This is not just a small immaterial difference in how we think about our intentions on the inside. When it comes to your actual physical manifestations, this makes *all of the difference* in your final results! Therefore, if you continue thinking about what you want while also simultaneously worrying about how it will come to you, the manifestations will take a long time to happen! They take a long time not because you are undeserving of what you ask for but because you'll attract more circumstances and events to be worried about instead of the desired manifestation.

Have you ever noticed how life seems to flow so smoothly for some people? They seem to get whatever they want without much fuss or thought! All they need to do is to *want* something on the inside, and somehow they get whatever they ask for a few days later in the form of a gift or a new opportunity. These individuals are usually regarded in our society as being lucky or "blessed by God" in some way. At the same time, these individuals often possess a kind of carefree and simplistic attitude towards life that has often been dismissed as being unsophisticated, naïve, or childish. I'm sure you'll be able to pinpoint at least one individual in your life who always has good things happening to him or her despite adopting a seemingly naïve attitude towards life. Could their mental attitudes hold the keys to physical manifestations?

After a thorough study of the science of manifestations, I am convinced of the link between one's mental attitudes and their outer results. Seemingly naïve individuals who adopt a simplistic attitude in life tend not to worry so much. They never fret over how things will happen to them. At the same time, they remain unattached to the outcome. This means that they are happy if things happen to them, but they are also all right if things do not work out the way they want. As a result, they often find things happening the way they want!

What would happen if we deliberately adopted this mental attitude? I'm not telling you to be unsophisticated or simplistic in your thinking but rather to give up all unnecessary worrisome and fearful thoughts that bog you down. Give all of that up. Give up the need to struggle or find your way, and just trust that the Universe already knows the best way for you. Let the Universe deliver that best way to you!

This new way of life takes some getting used to. Very often, we will not be able to keep ourselves physically still. We'll feel the incredible urge to "do something" to make things happen on the outside. But one valuable question we should ask before taking *any* physical action on the outside is this: Am I doing this out of fear/worry or out of inspiration/love? If the answer is the former, then it'll be in your highest interest not to act for now, for that will be your dominant vibration.

Before I realized this principle, I used to take action out of fear and worry all the time. I used to figure out ways and means to make more money, driven by a deep sense of fear that I would run out of money if I did not act in time or do something to "improve" the situation. My physical actions exhausted me and brought very little financial rewards. In fact, they drove me closer to where I did not want to go. My fear-based thinking and actions were the cause of my financial lack and I did not even realize it!

When I finally decided to "do nothing" until I felt the need to act out of inspiration or love, everything changed in an instant. That was when the Universe started providing for me. If I needed money, a check would come in at the right time to meet that need. If I needed something in my life, I would either get it as a gift or be given the means to purchase the item within the next week or so.

This new way of operating in the world sounds so magical precisely because it runs contrary to everything we have been taught, which is to "go out there and get it." If you'll just stop and ask yourself the question before you take any action, you'll be able to eliminate half or more of the actions you need to take from your life right now and still get more done.

This applies not only to the bigger things in life but also to the smaller ones. For example, I am feeling an urge right now to stop writing and make a call to book a birthday dinner for 10 this weekend. As this urge intensifies inside of me, I ask myself the question: Am I acting out of fear and worry or out of love and inspiration?

It turns out that my impulse is based on fear, because my logical self is worried that the restaurant will be fully booked and will run out of birthday cakes if I do not place my booking in time. I recognize it immediately as fear-based and lackful thinking and thus decide not to act until I feel truly inspired to do so. Remember that the Universe has endless ways to fulfill your intentions and desires! If you are aligned and allowing on the inside, then whatever venue you book will be just right for you. The food will be great, the service will be great, and there will be more than enough birthday cakes for everyone.

But things start to get awry when you allow yourself to act from a fear-based perspective. You may find that the line is busy no matter how many times you call or that there are no seats available (just as you feared) when you finally get through. Or you may meet with a grumpy service staff at the other end of the line. I have experienced this so many times in the past when I acted from a sense of fear, not realizing that my own vibrations were influencing my outer reality in tangible ways. When I changed the way I felt on the inside about something and only acted from that highest place of love and peace, the world around me reciprocated in kind.

Chapter Four
The Art of Reverse Manifestations

The greatest spiritual masters have repeatedly taught over the ages that the manifestation process is simple. All you have to do is to ask, and it will be given. Yet if the process is as simple as it sounds, why is it that so many people are still stranded without their manifestations? Why is it that so many are still struggling through life?

I used to be one of those who pondered this question. I thought there had to be some kind of a missing secret, a kind of mind hack or backdoor through which I could finally access the "real" powers of the Law of Attraction. Alas, after more than a decade of study and thousands of books and courses later…I realized that there are no missing secrets. Neither are there mind hacks or backdoors that we can access. All of these are romantic notions peddled by marketers to simply sell us more stuff. All we have to do—and this is the key to instant manifestations—is to *work on cultivating our own inner states.* When we remove all the negative feelings on the inside that are out of harmony with our original intentions, then our good will come incredibly quickly into our lives. Sadly, the reverse is also true. The longer we hold out and *demand* to see proof that this works *before* we are willing to change our inner states...the longer things will remain the same. It sounds unfair, but this is Universal Law.

I realize that when the spiritual masters said and taught something, they actually meant it in a literal sense. They were teaching it without any ulterior motives or ego. They have progressed beyond that stage! Therefore, the next time you come across any ancient spiritual message, whether it is in the form of a scripture or ancient mantra, first try to understand it *literally*. The literal meaning holds the keys to the original intentions of the teacher. Sometimes the teacher may attempt to communicate in parables, but beneath the parable is usually a straightforward message. This message, if applied in one's life, has the power to change the course of your life.

I can still remember the epiphany I had when I realized this is all real! I can still remember that exhilarating feeling I felt running through every fiber of my body when I realized that what the ancient spiritual masters taught were all true... every single word of it! Therefore, when Jesus says, "Ask and you shall receive," he really meant it quite literally. He was telling his followers (and anyone willing to listen) that if you are willing to ask, you will receive whatever you have asked for no matter what it is. Notice that Jesus did not say, "Ask and figure out how you shall get it, before you will receive it." Neither did he say, "Ask and then worry about how to get it!"

I'm sure if our Universe functioned according to the principles of hard work and struggle, this could have been the alternative words of Jesus. After all, this master teacher only wanted to teach his followers about the Universal truths as he perceived them and was willing to risk physical persecution to do so! The fact that Jesus said "Ask and you shall receive" in such a simple, straightforward manner points to the benevolent and magnanimous nature of the Universe. We are indeed lovingly supported in all of our endeavors.

My second epiphany in life came when I realized that no matter what these spiritual masters taught, I could always *prove their teachings for myself*. Since we are all living in the same Universe, these teachings should apply equally to everyone! When combined with my first realization that I should apply these truths faithfully, my physical world began to change right before my eyes. My life began to improve and straighten itself out with a speed that astonished even myself!

In the same way, you don't have to take any of these teachings at face value. *Prove them to yourself in your own life.* Give them a chance. I am telling you that they absolutely work, as evidenced by the transformed lives of hundreds of thousands of readers around the world who have taken the time and effort to put this into action. It does take some discipline and consistency in the beginning since we are deviating from our normal patterns of thought... but keep at it and you'll soon see results within a very short time. The saddest thing is to dismiss everything at the outset without even giving it a try. You really have nothing to lose and everything to gain.

I'll always remember what the great Ho'oponopono shaman Dr. Ihealeakala Hew Len said in one of his seminars. In his usual straightforward style, Dr. Hew Len said he will be "damned" if he ever "lied about to his students about any of this stuff!" In the same way, every teacher has come forth with the highest intentions to teach the truth. I must admit that I did not always think this way. I was always skeptical in the early days of my journey, so much so that I wondered if these spiritual teachers were just making things up to make us feel better! But understand that you do not always have to take their word for it. Prove their teachings in your own life and you'll realize the value of what they teach for yourself!

Now that we are on the same page, let us examine the five profoundly simple words echoed by the greatest spiritual teachers throughout the ages: ask and you shall receive. Look into any spiritual tradition and you see these five words repeated in their essence, albeit in different languages or forms. Why is that so? Does it hold the keys to our physical manifestations?

We can break this statement down into two parts. The first part consists of "asking." Contemporary spiritual teachers such as Abraham-Hicks have given their take on how to ask. Asking means holding an intention for something. I have written about intentions and their crucial role in many of my previous books so I will not repeat them here. What I want to focus on is the second part of the teaching that perplexes many: "and you shall receive." What do the great spiritual teachers mean when they jump straight from the asking to the receiving with absolutely nothing in between? Are there no intervening steps? Is it really as simple as asking on the inside and then receiving absolutely anything you have asked for?

The short answer to this question is yes. The process really *is* that simple. The long answer is somewhat more complicated and involves the concepts discussed in earlier chapters of this book. When the ancient spiritual teachers said "ask and you shall receive," they really meant it quite literally! They wanted you to hold an intention for something… and then *keep holding it purely* until you receive it! The last four words are key. We are supposed to hold an intention purely *until we receive it*. Unfortunately, the mass majority of the population have gone way ahead of themselves by asking for something and then sabotaging themselves in the interim by allowing negative thoughts and feelings to dominate their consciousness. This is certainly not what the ancient spiritual masters taught. When you are able to hold an intention for what you want purely, the very thing you ask for comes into your life almost immediately with no delay or time lag. Lester Levenson wrote about such spontaneous manifestation experiences in his books, and so have Dr. David Hawkins in his book *Letting Go*. When a pure intention was held on the inside for a particular food item at the restaurant, it was brought over by the waitress almost instantly with no outer delay! While we may wonder how that can even be possible, let's not forget that it is in accordance with what the spiritual masters have always taught: ask and you shall receive.

My intention for this book is to teach readers an easy way to apply this manifestation principle. I call it the art of *reverse manifestations*. This means that instead of viewing the manifestation process from where you are at the moment, I would like to invite you to view it from the end. Imagine yourself right at the very end of the manifestation process where the final physical manifestation has already occurred. This in itself is nothing new since many spiritual teachers have advocated the importance of feeling "as if" something is already true for us. But this technique goes beyond just feeling "as if." It actually turns the entire manifestation process around on its head. We start with the end in mind and *stay there*, just as the spiritual masters throughout the ages have taught and done for themselves.

One downside of feeling "as if" is that we usually need to use lots of mental energy and effort to conjure up those feelings. We usually have to try very hard to sustain the intensity of those feelings. One reason why students of this material often abandon the practice of visualization is because of the amount of mental effort it takes! In the beginning, visualizations and feeling "as if" may seem fun and energizing to an individual. However, the longer one tries them without any evidence of their physical manifestations in sight, the greater the tendency to feel discouraged and skeptical about the whole process. That is when self-doubt and desperation start to seep in. It is these negative feelings that keep your physical manifestations at bay! Let me repeat it as this is important: It is these *negative feelings* that creep in that keep your physical manifestations from happening. If you found a way to eliminate all (or most) of these feelings from your inner state, then your physical manifestations will happen very quickly.

Visualization usually works for the "small things" because our negative feelings of worry and self-doubt are not as intense. Also, because of our own expectations, "small" things take a faster time to manifest for us. Therefore, we do not have to visualize for as long to see small manifestations take place. However, visualization usually falls flat on its face for the "bigger" things that we ask for. This is not because visualization does not work; it is very effective as a manifestation tool. However, even an effective manifestation tool *cannot function* well under the presence of repeated negative feelings or thoughts.

This is why it is so important to find a way to handle these negative feelings and thoughts as they arise. We do so not by fighting or suppressing them, but by using various clever techniques to dissolve or keep them away. In fact, most of my books are about dealing with the physical resistance in the manifestation process, because this is the part that most people trip themselves up. When you dissolve any resistance or disharmonious elements in the process, then your manifestations *have to happen spontaneously for you*, no matter what you ask for.

So the first step to applying reverse manifestations is simply this: We start from the opposite side. We begin with the end in mind. Form a clear mental picture of what you would like to manifest and how it would feel like when the final manifestation has taken place. This does not always have to be in the form of a mental image that you hold in your mind. It can also be the strong and intense feelings that you feel when you finally have something. The good news here is that I will *not* be asking you to hold on to these feelings repeatedly for long. You will not be asked to conjure any of these good feelings up. Instead, you will be led through a process to feel and experience these good feelings spontaneously on their own.

The process of reverse manifestations is one where we begin with the end in mind. However, contrary to conventional wisdom, we do not start at the end and then figure out a way to get from the final manifestation to where we are now. There is no "figuring out" what you have to do. We are not trying to reverse-engineer the process or to come up with ways through which you can manifest something by working backwards. Recall that none of these physical actions are needed in the creative process. Deciding how something will come to you is not your job unless you also have a clear intent on how you want something to come to you. So we will leave figuring out the specifics to the Universe and focus entirely on our part of the equation—deciding what we want and maintaining our undivided focus on it.

Chapter Five
The Pure Essence of Joy In Our Final Manifestations

The first step of the reverse manifestations process is to be in touch with the pure essence of joy in our final manifestations. If that sounds like a mouthful, stay with me and I'll take you through the whole process. But just for now, think about something you would like to manifest in your life. It may be a tangible physical object (such as a car or a beautiful piece of jewelry) or an intangible experience (a skydiving trip, a seminar, a vacation, or being in an ideal relationship). Whatever your manifestation intention may be, gently bring it to your mind right now.

I usually recommend that we start with tangible physical objects on the first few tries and here's why. When we intend a physical item into our lives, the process is fairly straightforward as we are only dealing with a single standalone item/intention. When we intend a particular situation into our lives, the situation usually comprises of multiple intentions. As you become more proficient at handling standalone intentions, you'll become more comfortable with the subtleties of handling multiple intentions. Also, when we set an intention for a physical item, it is easy to see whether results have occurred in our lives. The fact that the object manifests itself means we have been successful in our attempt! On the other hand, it is not as easy to assess whether our intangible manifestations have taken place. Students often tell me that they get one part of their intentions but not the other part, or things did not really turn out exactly the way they wanted. Once again, as you become more proficient at manifesting single intentions, you'll automatically figure out how to blend multiple intentions together into your life experience.

So just for now, choose a single intention to focus on. We will be using the same intention throughout all the exercises in this book so you can have your first manifestation set up even before you finish reading this book! In just a moment, you will close your eyes and picture yourself enjoying the final manifestation. If it is a physical object you are asking for, see yourself using the item and enjoying it immensely. If it is an intangible experience that you desire, see yourself going through the experience or a particular aspect of the experience.

Now here is where things will differ from conventional manifestation wisdom. Some self-help teachers will ask you to feel *as if*, which is to feel the feelings of your final manifestation as vividly and intensely in your body as possible. While this is certainly an effective way to manifest, I have also observed that it is a practice that can be difficult to sustain for extended periods of time, especially in the absence of any physical manifestations! In place of that, I have found a much smoother and nonresistant path. Here's what you should do: as you close your eyes and bring the intention to mind, zoom in on *particular aspects of the final manifestation* that please you greatly.

For example, if I am trying to manifest my dream car, I would close my eyes and imagine the beautiful, sleek lines of the car. That is one *aspect* of the car that pleases me greatly and thrills me to no end when I think about it. You may also focus on how wonderful it feels to have your hands wrapped around the exquisite steering wheel. If I were intending a watch, I may hone in on a single aspect and imagine the minute hand sweeping gracefully across the polished watch face.

Let the particular aspect that pleases you greatly *present itself to you*. This is not a random exercise where we simply choose any aspect of the item to focus upon. Rather, choose something that excites you. What do you like so much about the item you're trying to manifest? What is it about the item that excites you? Why do you want to have it in the first place? Do you appreciate how it looks or how it functions? What aspect of it attracts you? All these questions can be asked to identify the one single aspect of the final manifestation that thrills you greatly.

When I think about my dream car, my thoughts automatically drift to how beautifully constructed the car is. I feel an immense sense of appreciation over how finely engineered the car is. While I don't "see" a particular part of the car in my mind's eye, I can *feel* a sense of appreciation and joy for the engineering of the car. Thus, that is the aspect that I focus upon in this exercise. Similarly, when I think about my dream watch, I also feel an immense sense of appreciation for how finely engineered the watch is. That is the aspect of the watch that I connect to in these exercises.

You'll find that different people are drawn to different aspects of their manifestations. Some people may appreciate the physical attributes and beauty of certain items, while others may appreciate the fine engineering and thought that goes into their design. Yet another may appreciate the feelings that are associated with their use. Therefore, while we may sometimes ask for the same things, the aspects that we appreciate may be very different. Take some time now to identify the major aspect that attracts your attention and captures your imagination the most. What is it that is so pleasing to you about your final manifestation? Which aspect of it attracts and draws you greatly? Which aspect of it makes you love and dream?

When you zoom in and focus on a particular aspect of your final manifestation that pleases you greatly, a few things immediately happen. First, you notice a pure, spontaneous, and powerful sense of joy in your being. This is what I refer to as the *pure essence of joy* in our final manifestations. What is interesting about this sense of pure joy is that you will find it in *all* of your desires in life. If you repeat the process above with another of your desired manifestations and really get in touch with this pure essence of joy…you'll find the feelings of joy to be the same *no matter what physical object you're trying to manifest.*

When you connect with this sense of pure joy, you connect with the divine forces of the Universe that brought the item into being in the first place. So when you connect and feel this pure joy when you think about your dream car, you connect with that sense of inspiration and love that caused the car to be designed in the first place! When you connect with the essence of pure joy for a particular piece of jewelry, you experience the same unbridled joy that the jewelry craftsman had in bringing his design to fruition. You experience that exact sense of love, the Universal force of inspiration, which brought that design from the ethereal into the physical. This is a highly significant piece of the manifestation process because you are *tapping into the very same power that creates worlds!* You are tapping into the powerful energy that brought that creation into this world in the first place!

Take some time to connect with and recognize the pure essence of joy in your final manifestations. You'll find that no matter which item you apply this process to, you'll feel the *same unbridled, blossoming joy* once you focus intently on the particular aspect that pleases you the most. That's because all of our physical desires and intentions represent our quest for greater happiness and joy in our lives. No matter what you ask for in life, you want it because you believe you will become happier in the having of it. Therefore, *pure joy* is at the basis of everything that you seek. Pure joy *is* the purest essence of your final manifestations!

Powerful energies are harnessed when you focus on the pure joy underlying your intentions and final manifestations. You are cutting through all of that negative energy, letting all of your resistant feelings go in the moment and just focusing purely on your intention. When you do so, you are "asking" in the purest possible form. That is stage one of the creative process as we discussed earlier. This is asking in its purest possible form with absolutely no resistant or contradictory thoughts. When you "ask" in such a pure and powerful way by focusing your intentions on the most joyful aspects of what you are asking for…the physical manifestations *have to come,* and they will come very quickly!

This is not a process to be rushed. Once again, you do not attempt to conjure up artificial feelings of joy in any of this. This is not an exercise in using your imagination. Instead, it is about reconnecting with a part of yourself that has always been there. It is like meeting with an old friend after a long while, and finding all the good memories and pleasant feelings flooding back to you. You do not have to make any of those feelings up; they just come rushing back to you all at once! In the same way, once you connect with that joyful aspect of your final manifestation that pleases you greatly…those feelings of spontaneous joy will come rushing to you all at once without any conscious intervention on your part! The feeling will be so strong, so intense, and so pure!

In my early days when I did this exercise, I often found myself trembling and shaking in my seat when waves of profound joy surged over me. The feeling can get very intense, but it is always warm and never uncomfortable. The more intense the feeling gets, the more pleasant and energized one feels on the inside. So this exercise will not be uncomfortable or unsafe for you although your physical body may take some time to adjust to these higher vibrations. In my first few years of doing these exercises, I often felt so much love and joy surge through my body that my eyes would fill up with tears and I would start swaying in my chair. All of this is natural. Let everything that happens be all right. Know that you are connecting with very pure Universal essence and energy here. In fact, you are tapping into this energy and letting it flow through your being.

I like to use the mantra "higher and higher" to remind myself that no matter how joyful I feel, I can always heighten and intensify this sense of immense joy. Of course, this analogy is not entirely accurate. Universal energy just *is*, and there is no duality in something that is already so intense and pure. There is no lesser joy or more joy. There is only joy. However, what causes us to perceive "lesser" or "more" joy in our physical bodies as we go through this experience is the unconscious physical resistance that we have picked up. For example, my body used to be constantly tensed up from decades of resistant thought and worrying. When I tried this exercise to connect with the essence of pure joy, my physical body could not keep up with the energy that was going through my systems, hence the tears and tremors. As you repeat these exercises and acclimatize yourself to the higher vibrations of love, peace, and joy, these feelings will become more natural to you.

Therefore, in the beginning, I like to use the phrase "higher and higher" to remind myself that there is always more physical resistance that I can consciously let go of. I can relax just a bit more in the moment to allow more of that joy to flow through me. I am even feeling it now so intensely in my body as I write these words, as goosebumps well up all over my body. It is a very pleasant and euphoric sensation.

I would like you to devote the rest of today to connecting with this pure essence of joy in your final manifestations. Think about your intention in general and then hone in on one particular aspect that pleases you the most. As you hold this aspect in your mind and appreciate it, feel those sensations well up all over your body. Feel them intensely in your body. This feeling is similar to what one gets when they gently pet their cat. Notice how you feel when you are petting your beloved animal. Your thoughts are wholly focused on how much you love and appreciate your animal. You appreciate the nice coat of fur it has. You appreciate the joyful company it provides you. You appreciate all the fun times you had together. The list goes on and on and on! In the same way, you are petting your final manifestations! You are appreciating the positive aspects of that final manifestation and letting it please you greatly.

Notice how it is totally impossible to feel any negative feelings when you are fully connected to this pure essence of joy. Notice how all the negative feelings of worry, fear, and desperation just melt away completely. You simply cannot hold two thoughts at the same time or be immersed in two inner states at the same time! It is always one or the other. Hence, when you immerse yourself in these powerful positive energies of joy and peace, you'll find all the resistant thoughts and feelings completely fading away. This is an important key to the final manifestations because physical shifts can only happen when these nonresistant feelings go away.

Spend the rest of today intensifying those feelings. Notice how pure and unconditional the feelings are. Remind yourself that you can always go "higher and higher," that you can always feel more and more of that loving energy. Very often, people hold themselves back and restrict themselves when something "feels too good." They are even secretly worried whether it is sinful to feel this pleasurable and good! Let all of these resistant thoughts out of your mind. Let your self-imposed limitations and self-consciousness go. No one has to know that you're sitting there in your office chair and feeling this good! You may even let out a sigh or moan in the process!

Focus on intensifying these feelings and experiencing them for longer periods at a time. I have not found any adverse effects from immersing myself in these feelings for hours on end. You'll find that these feelings do not tire you out. On the contrary, they are self-sustaining and energize you immensely. The more you put yourself in alignment with the purest essence of who you are, the more you feel this sense of Universal oneness, the more in tune you will be with the Universal forces that we are part of. Feeling this pure energy has the added benefit of correcting many physical ailments or symptoms in the body. The energy that you feel running through your body is infinite Universal intelligence, and in its presence, everything that has gone "wrong" as a result of resistant thought patterns straighten themselves out!

Start with one intention. Focus on one or two aspects of it and notice the pure essence of joy contained within. When you do so, you are connecting with the power that creates worlds. You transcend the boundaries of space and time to connect with everyone who had a hand in creating this manifestation with you, even people from the future who will bring your desired item to you. Stay with these feelings. Immerse yourself wholeheartedly in them for longer periods at a time and notice the spontaneous dissolving of any resistant, disharmonious thoughts. Once you do so, your manifestations are settled!

Chapter Six
Higher And Higher, Better And Better

Notice how blissful you felt when you connected with the pure essence of joy in your final manifestations. Everything felt so right and smooth with no contradictory feelings or resistant thoughts. The absence of resistant thoughts about your intended manifestations is the reason why you felt so good and energized during the process. Resistant thoughts about whether our intentions will come true for us lead to negative feelings of discouragement and self-doubt, all of which drain us physically and emotionally when held for prolonged periods of time in our consciousness. When we let all of those resistant feelings go, we experience immediate physical relief...and that is only the beginning!

When you connect to the pure essence of joy within your final manifestations, everything works out smoothly for you. You do not have to worry about how you will get what you want, neither do you have to fuss over the physical steps to get there. Notice how all these worrisome thoughts about the specifics just melted away when you connected with that pure essence of joy within. Let the Universe handle the logistics because it is equipped to do a far better job than you! The Universe knows all of the parameters involved and the personal preferences of everyone who is related to your intention. Let it take care of all the nitty-gritty details, satisfying the needs of everyone while you focus purely on what you would like to manifest.

The most commonly asked question at this point is, "Is there anything else I have to do?"

Spiritual masters have often taught that there is nothing more you need to do and that everything is settled in the moment you hold a pure intention (ask) for something. The same applies here when you use the reverse manifestation process. Once you have held your intention purely and connected with the pure essence of joy in your final manifestations… *there is nothing more you have to do.* Leave all of the details and logistics up to the Universe and just revel in the fun of your newfound life! Find joy in living your life instead of worrying about how things you ask for will come to you. Live fully in each moment instead of worrying about perceived "problems" and "issues" from the future. Those can just as easily be solved by following these Universal principles. No amount of brain activity and intellect will allow you to dictate every single minute detail in your life, so why not leave it up to a higher power?

If you insist on *doing* something, then let it be this: Whenever you have the opportunity or free time, consciously connect and feel the pure essence of joy present in your final manifestations. For a start, you can do so three times a day. Set aside three quiet periods a day where you can just be with yourself. Allow yourself to become really comfortable, close your eyes, and then connect with the pure essence of joy present in your final manifestations. I would devote around 5 to 10 minutes for each session. Your intention for these sessions is not to make anything happen on the outside but solely to feel the pure joy that is present in your final manifestations right now, *in this moment.*

Remember that anytime you try "hard" to achieve something or make something happen, you are working against the Universal flow. You are trying to insist that things come to you through a particular path or method. Let go of the need to try hard or even try at all! Let go of any long-held beliefs about struggle you may have inherited from your parents. The struggle along the path is always optional. Take the path of least resistance on the inside. This means becoming very still, going within, and connecting with that sense of pure joy and peace that has always been there. You'll find that the feelings intensify for you each time you try this exercise because there is truly no limit to how good things can be on the inside! The mantra "higher and higher" comes in handy here. As things *feel* better on the inside, your outer circumstances will improve accordingly. Our outer world is nothing but a mirror of our inner state.

I always go into each "connecting" session with an open mind and a childlike sense of curiosity, wondering how much better I can feel in the upcoming session. Your feelings will give you a clue as to how close you are to your final manifestations. When you feel *really* good about something as you think about it with absolutely no sense of resistance, it means the physical manifestation is *really* close! Expect it in your physical reality soon and look out for it! You will be given hints and clues by the Universe. On the other hand, if you still feel some form of inner discord or disharmony when you think about your goals and intentions, it means you are further away from your physical manifestations. You're further away not because you are undeserving of what you have asked for, but because of the contradictory thoughts and feelings that you still allow yourself to hold.

Notice that I used the word "allow" in the previous sentence. When physical manifestations do not show up in our lives, there is a tendency to ascribe the blame to various third parties—to the economy, our bosses, jealous colleagues for sabotaging our efforts, uncooperative clients, and so on. But know that *none of these matter* if you are truly in alignment with your highest self! When you are in the Universal flow, none of these external factors matter one bit. No one will be able to sabotage you even if they wanted to! You will truly be under divine protection wherever you go. This is why prayers for protection work if you use them with a pure intent (out of love, and not out of fear or spite). You will be so vibrationally incompatible with individuals holding differing intentions that they will be taken out of your physical life experience completely! This is the fundamental Law of Attraction at work.

I remember a lady at work who used to make others look bad to get ahead. She would frequently point out various flaws in the work of others to the higher-ups in the hopes of gaining their favor. I was often amazed while working with this lady how her poisonous arrows missed me so narrowly! For example, I would uncover a mistake just before she had the chance to report it or that something else would happen to catch her attention at the right moment. That was in the beginning when I was still integrating these Universal principles into my life. As I focused and connected more with my higher intentions, I was miraculously taken out of the situation a year later. While I was initially sad to leave that position (as there were many aspects about it that I liked), I realized I had also been holding strong intentions to be free from any interactions with this lady. The Universe freed me from an emotionally draining and negative situation without me having to do it myself.

Prove these principles to yourself in your daily life by connecting with the pure essence of joy thrice a day and intensifying those good feelings each time. The 5 to 10 minutes you spend on each session will shift your vibrations drastically such that you will no longer be vibrating at the same low level of worry or fear as in the past. Notice how differently the world responds to you when you step out and various opportunities start coming your way. At first, there is a tendency to dismiss all these good happenings as mere "good luck" or coincidence. But keep at it and you'll find them becoming regular occurrences in your life. That's when you will fully awaken to the power of tending to your inner states.

There is no value in blaming another when your physical manifestations do not happen for you. In my work, I have heard all sorts of excuses that people give when things do not manifest for them, ranging from "some secret steps are withheld from me" to "they have priced this so high I cannot afford to buy it!"

Anytime you feel the urge to blame any external factors for your lack of physical results, pause for a moment and let those negative feelings go. Drop them without engaging in them any further. The more you insist on why you *cannot* have something, the more you'll be at the mercy of those external circumstances. What you're effectively intending is for the external circumstances and obstacles to remain the same or even grow bigger in your face. That's why spiritual teachers have repeatedly taught that whenever we say "no" to something out of frustration or fear, we are actually attracting more of it into our lives by virtue of our continued attention to the unwanted. Let all of that go and focus purely on your desires! Instead of insisting that these obstacles exist, spend your time and energy focusing on how good your final manifestations would feel like to you.

The good news is that once you understand the nature of the Universe, you'll also intuitively understand that manifestations are an inside job. The only thing that prevents what you want from coming to you are your negative feelings such as fear, worry, resentment, blame, undeservingness, or guilt. Get all these feelings out of your consciousness and you would have closed the gap between your current moment and the actual physical manifestation. Hence, the journey you have to take is an inner one. If you could convince yourself to take this journey and "close the gap" by the end of today, then your physical manifestations could happen by the end of today and latest by tomorrow!

Some people just need a longer time to convince themselves to let go of all the negative feelings surrounding their intentions. We have been conditioned to look to our physical world for *external* evidence and hang on to those as if they were the whole truth.

As I look back on my own journey, I realize that my first few manifestations happened painstakingly slowly because I stubbornly held on to my feelings of undeservingness the whole time. I wanted to attract my dream car very badly and yet at the same time, I could not get rid of all my associated feelings of undeservingness and self-doubt. I now know that these feelings of undeservingness are largely the result of social conditioning. "Who am I to drive such a car? What would others think if I drove this car? What if I cannot afford to maintain it?" All these negative thoughts kept recurring in my head whenever I tried to focus on my desires, which is why I had such a difficult time manifesting my intention on the outside! If I had found a way to rid myself of all those negative thoughts, my manifestations would have happened in a matter of days or weeks instead of years. The physical manifestation would have been instantaneous.

Right now, you probably perceive a number of obstacles standing between you and your desires. The good news is that dealing with these obstacles is not your job. The Universe always has a bird's-eye view of the whole forest and is able to see the trails that will lead you to where you want to be. Your job is to first take the inner journey on the inside…to get yourself to that place on the inside where you feel the pure, unadulterated joy of your final manifestations in the now moment. When you get to that peaceful place of love and peace on the inside and *stay there often,* that is when your physical manifestations will happen on the outside. In the next chapter, I'll talk about how the Universe calls us forth to our greater good.

Chapter Seven
The Universe Always Nudges You In The Right Direction

The Universe always calls you forth towards your greater good. I have been searching for a car for the past six months. The thought of haggling with car dealers and handling the documentation for my old car left me unmotivated to start my search. In the past, I would have ignored these negative feelings on the inside and reluctantly embarked on my car-hunting journey on the outside. But not this time around. As a student of these metaphysical principles, I know that whenever I feel even the slightest bit of resistance on the inside, it means that I am not yet ready for my physical manifestations on the outside. Acting from this state of fear/confusion instead of clarity would only cause unwanted manifestations down the road.

Recall the question from Chapter 3 that can be used to reduce your workload or to-do list by half: Am I taking this action out of fear and worry, or out of inspiration and love? This question is all it takes to reveal your true feelings behind your physical actions.

Whenever I felt the urgency to look for a new car, I realized that I was acting from a sense of fear that time was running out and that I would not be able to get the best price for my existing car. Each time these thoughts arose, I would calm myself down by repeating the following affirmation, one which I learned from New Thought author Catherine Ponder: Everything happens for me in divine timing, and it is so!

Each time I felt the urge to go out there and "do something," I assessed whether the need for action stemmed from fear or inspiration. I felt the impulse to act numerous times over the course of six months. But upon a closer examination of my own thoughts, I realized that I was really acting out of a sense of desperation and worry rather than from a place of love. I let those desperate feelings go the moment they came up, and I repeat the affirmation to myself.

One thing I did feel inspired to do was browse the Internet for car listings. This action felt natural for me and it did not make me feel uneasy or resistant on the inside. Searching the Internet for suitable car listings represented the *path of least resistance* for me, and that was exactly what I did.

It always helps to look for the path of least resistance no matter what you are trying to manifest in your outer experience. You may be looking for a new house, a new relationship, or even a new car like myself. What you are looking for does not matter. The Universe always knows the fastest and most direct way to reach your goal if you let it guide you!

The path of least resistance is the one that feels the most natural to you in the current moment. It is the one that has no inertia or discord attached to it. When I take the path of least resistance, everything feels effortless and light. I feel energized by what I am doing as if the Universe is calling me forth to the next step, and then the next. Whenever I doubt whether it is the right path to take or second-guess myself, I know I am not following the path of least resistance. That is probably a path conjured by my logical mind, which wants me to take a particular path to "make something happen" on the outside.

Look for the path of least resistance in every situation. It is always present and always there no matter how dire the situation may be. However, the path of least resistance may not always seem to be the most logical or the most direct. Although surfing the Internet for car listings was the easiest and most natural thing for me to do back then, I still had that small voice at the back of my head saying, "Shouldn't you be going out there and physically looking at cars instead of just browsing the Internet all day?" You get the idea. Our logical ego mind can be so insidious in getting us to act that it bombards us with baseless fearful thoughts all day. Recognize these thoughts for what they are: a lack of faith in these Universal forces.

After six months of browsing the Internet for suitable car listings, I finally saw a listing that caught my eye. The car was in great condition, had a great history, and was one of the few models I was considering. The only caveat was that the dealership was at the other end of town, far from where I lived. However, I had this strange impulse to drive across town even though it was late on a Sunday afternoon. I did not even know whether they would be open! This time around, my impulse to act stemmed from inspiration and not fear. I felt inspired to drive down directly and did just that.

It took me an hour to get to the dealership. When I arrived, I was disappointed to find that all the shops along that street were closed on a quiet Sunday afternoon. There was not a single person in sight. I drove right past the given address and saw the shutters drawn.

For some strange reason, I felt inspired to circle the block once again. Instead of feeling disappointed that the place was closed, I had an inner knowing that it would be open! That was strange since all physical signs showed otherwise. There were at least 10 other dealerships along that street and every single one of them was closed. I circled the block a second time and this time around, I felt inspired to make a turn into a narrow pathway. That was when I saw it.

Wedged between two shuttered shop units was a small transparent glass door, along with a small flashing sign on top that said "OPEN." It felt like a scene right out of a science fiction movie! I felt goosebumps running all over my body as a strong sense of inner confirmation came over me.

My delight quickly turned into disappointment when I noticed that the shop sold mattresses and children's beds rather than cars! However, my disappointment quickly gave way to amazement as the sole salesperson in the shop explained that due to the economic downturn, they have started selling bedding products as well. He assured me that I was at the right place.

I took the car for a test drive and purchased it on the spot after verifying its history. The dealership was willing to handle the trade-in as well. More importantly, the salesperson was honest and a deal was quickly reached. Even though I've been a student of these Universal principles for a long time, I couldn't believe how smoothly everything went. After six months of waiting, it took me just one day to find and purchase my desired car. The Universe took care of everything for me in divine timing.

Can you imagine how much time and effort I would have spent if I physically went out and looked at cars for the past six months? I would undoubtedly have wasted hundreds of hours of my precious time scouring the car dealerships and negotiating with various salespeople. That was what I would have done if I had not trusted the Universe to orchestrate everything for me. I might even have ended up with the shorter end of the stick had I taken this more arduous route!

Let The Universe Lead You!

What I have described above requires a certain degree of faith and trust in the Universe. It may not be easy to see the whole picture especially from our current vantage points, but we must always trust that the Universe knows better. The Universe has a complete view of the situation and perceives none of the physical limitations that we do. At the same time, the Universe is always nudging us towards the path of our physical manifestations. Our job is to act on the cues that are given to us.

There have been countless stories throughout the ages about how businessmen have made a fortune by acting on their seemingly illogical hunches. The most famous story involves Conrad Hilton, founder of the Hilton chain of hotels. Mr. Hilton had bid on a Chicago property in a sealed bidding exercise for $165,000 but had a nagging hunch to change his bid to $180,000 the next morning. He did so and outbid his nearest bidder by a mere $200.

Notice what happened in Mr. Hilton's case. The Universe did not just nudge him to increase his bid out of the blue. He had to signal his intention for the Chicago property by placing a bid for it first. Once he held an intention to buy that property, the Universe supported him in his endeavor by revealing to him the path of least resistance. In his case, the path of least resistance would have been to bid for the hotel and the Universe showed him the "right" price to offer for it.

What about the other parties who placed their bids for the same property? Didn't they hold similar intentions to own the property? This is where the purity of our intentions and the ability to focus on our desired outcomes come in handy.

Over the years, I've had the good fortune of working with entrepreneurs from diverse industries and backgrounds. One thing I noticed about top-performing entrepreneurs is their uncanny ability to control their inner states and focus *singularly* on their desired outcome, unaffected by what goes on around them. They are usually so clear on what they want that they will go as far as to ignore conventional wisdom. To outsiders who do not know any better, these individuals seem to be acting recklessly and taking on disproportionate amounts of risk. But the fact is that they are actually acting with great prudence. These individuals know the value of their Universal guidance system and have come to trust in it over time. On the contrary, an individual who allows himself to be swayed by physical evidence, or by the whims and fancies of others, *is* acting recklessly, for he does not hold on clearly to the inner vision of what he wants.

As we close this chapter, I would like you to identify a single path of least resistance that you can take today. This is not a logical exercise and you do not have to search too hard for it. All you have to do is to relax, think about what you want, and see if you feel *inspired* to take any action in relation to your goal. If there are no "paths" in sight, then just let go and enjoy your day. There is nothing you have to do at the moment and you might as well enjoy your time!

However, if there is an action that you feel particularly inspired to do right now with regards to your intentions, go and do it no matter how illogical or irrelevant it seems.

The Universe works in mysterious ways but it always leads us to our higher good. Never once have I been in trouble as a result of following a path of least resistance. On the other hand, I have sometimes been in hot soup when I refused to follow the paths that were presented to me! The struggle along the journey is always optional. We struggle only when we refuse to take the path of least resistance and instead try to use our logic and intellect to figure things out.

I have come to appreciate my Universal guidance system for pointing me in the right direction at crucial crossroads in my life. For example, there was a period when I was inexplicably "addicted" to reading magazines and would buy one magazine after another from the newsstands. My new behavior seemed illogical to me at that time but I have learned to, as Louise Hay put it, "follow my inner ding!" It turns out that my period of binge reading magazines gave me some valuable business insights and led me to rethink my business model in profitable ways.

The Universe is trying to lead you towards your greater good in every moment. All you have to do is to turn inwards and take the path of least resistance that is presented to you. If you'll just take the first small step, then the next one and the next will become increasingly clearer to you. As Martin

Luther King Jr. puts it so eloquently, "You don't have to see the whole staircase, just take the first step."

Take the first step of the staircase that feels just right for you, but till then...be still and listen for that inner nudge within!

Chapter Eight
You Always Get the Vibrational Essence of What You Ask For

We live in a vibrational Universe. This means that the Universe does not communicate with us at the level of physical words or actions. Rather, it communicates through a series of electrical impulses that we interpret as feelings, emotions, and thoughts. The Universe picks up on our intent in a similar manner through our thoughts and feelings. Any thought or feeling held on the inside is instantly "received" and acted upon by the Universe depending on the "vibrational frequency" of that thought.

The outmoded view is that there is some higher being standing by, always watching over us and observing our physical actions, ready to dish out the appropriate rewards and punishments accordingly. If this were the case, one would always be rewarded for their good deeds and punished for their "sins" in life. Yet we do not observe this to be the case. Bad things happen to good people and "bad" people often get away scot-free. Why is this so? There has to be a higher explanation.

Readers are often surprised when I point out that we don't always get what we ask for. Rather, we *always* get the *vibrational essence* of what we ask for, every single time. As you apply these spiritual principles to your life, you'll notice this to be true. Telling the Universe what you want in physical words does not ensure that you'll eventually end up with what you want. Therefore, there is no need to repeat your affirmations or goals over and over again in the hope of sending a clear signal to some higher being. The Universe has picked up on your desires the very first time you held those intentions! The Universe does not work at the level of mere physical words or actions.

It is the *feelings* you hold on the inside (the energetic vibrations arising from your intentions) that determine what physically manifests on the outside. Therefore, if you ask for more money but hold on to fearful and worrisome thoughts each time you think about money, guess what will be the vibrational essence of what you ask for? That's right: although you are asking for more money in words, the vibrational essence of your desires is *completely different* from that of financial abundance. What you consciously ask for and how you unconsciously allow yourself to feel on the inside is of two worlds. Since you are always given the vibrational essence of what you ask for, you will simply create more reasons and conditions to make you feel worried about your finances in life.

I wish to devote some time here to explain the concept of vibrational essence because it is an esoteric subject that is often misunderstood. The good news is that life becomes a breeze once you fully understand the vibrational nature of our Universe. Not only will your physical manifestations happen way faster than before with hardly any time lag, but you'll also be able to accurately pinpoint why some of your desires have not manifested in the past. You'll always be able to find out what is holding them back. I can assure you that it will always be some form of a mismatch between how you feel on the inside and the vibrational essence of what you are asking for.

Since everything around us is made up of energy, every tangible object or intangible situation comprises of corresponding vibrational frequencies. Similarly, *thinking* about (focusing our thought energies on) a particular object or situation creates a matching vibrational frequency within us. These vibrational frequencies are interpreted by us as our feelings and emotions. When we think about a joyful situation in life, we *feel* the corresponding vibrational essence of the situation and, as a result, feel happy on the inside. Conversely, when we think about something that makes us angry, we *feel* the corresponding vibrations of the situation and feel unhappy.

When we think about our intentions, however, things become less straightforward. We may be thinking about a seemingly positive intention, but due to the emotional baggage and social conditioning surrounding that intention, our associated feelings and emotions may not always be as positive.

One good example is holding an intention for greater financial abundance. While that in itself is a positive, uplifting intention, the subject of money is often a source of distress for many. Therefore, one's thoughts about money often revolve around worrisome subjects of saving it, not losing it and making more of it.

Notice how you feel on the inside when you think about money. Does thinking about your finances make you feel joyful or constricted on the inside? If thinking about your money makes you feel pure joy, then I know (without even having met you) that money flows easily and effortlessly into your life. You always have all the money you need, when you need it. On the other hand, if thinking about your finances makes you feel constricted and tight in the chest, then I also know that there is a lack of money in your life right now.

Most readers will be tempted to say, "Oh, it is easy for you to feel pure joy about money because you have lots of it right now!" Doing so will be falling into the trap that have caught many others along the same path.

While it is true that having *some* money in the first place does allow one to feel better about their finances, the big secret is that *you can feel good about anything in your life independent of outer, physical circumstances.* You may have nothing in the bank right now, but if you found a way to connect with that sense of pure joy and abundance when you think about the fortune you seek...then the money (or whatever you ask for) *has to show up*! This is Universal Law!

This is also the point that I struggled with the hardest when I first learned these Universal principles. Abraham-Hicks would be making this same point over and over again in all of their books, tapes, and courses until I became sick and tired of hearing it. My retort was always the same, "Oh yeah, it is easy for you to feel good because you already have lots of money!"

My response ignored the fundamental basis of their teachings, which is this: You do *not* need the physical evidence of something to feel good! This means that you can feel good about money *even though* you do not physically have it at the moment. You can feel good about all the things you're asking for even though they have not physically appeared in your life right now. And guess what, the moment you feel good about them and connect to the pure essence of joy within them...*that* is when all of it starts flowing into your life.

How do you think the self-made tycoons and businessmen became financially wealthy? Did they always have money in their pockets? Did the money somehow appear in their bank accounts? Absolutely not! Every single one of them had to start from a place where they had very little money and make their way out of those circumstances.

The biggest skill that each of these individuals have mastered is to *stop* focusing on the physical lack of money and instead think about something else that energizes them. Bill Gates, Steve Jobs, and many others of the same era immersed themselves wholeheartedly in the development of computers and software that they believed would change the world. These entrepreneurs invested all their mental energy in things that energized and made them feel good, instead of dwelling on things that made them feel not as good. As you can see, their single-mindedness has paid off tremendously.

One of my favorite pastimes in my early days was reading the autobiographies of successful people across various fields. As a young teenager, I was always dying to know that one elusive success secret, the common thread that ran through all of their successes. If success was to be found in a particular industry, I reasoned that I should perhaps start my career in that industry. Unfortunately (or fortunately) for me, I realized after reading my 50th success story that there wasn't a single factor that accounted for success in life. These people were making money in all types of economies. They came from diverse educational and family backgrounds. They were of different ages. However, every single one of them had an undying belief in something that energized them greatly. They were totally consumed by the intensity of this overriding belief! It is only years later after learning about these metaphysical principles that I realize this is exactly what makes the difference in our outer results—the ability to place our singular focus on the things we want to the exclusion of everything else.

If you wish to become an effective manifestor, you must cultivate a heightened sense of awareness about how *you feel on the inside.* Most people live their lives completely oblivious to how they feel on the inside. We have been taught to suppress our feelings and not expose them to the outside world. As a result, many of us have learned to completely ignore our feelings or even deny their existence. Others live in an outer-directed manner, letting their inner states be dictated by whatever is happening in their lives at the moment.

As I write this, the car that I wrote about in the previous chapter is now sitting in my garage. After six months of me literally "doing nothing," the Universe led me to my ideal car within a single day. Three days later, I drove the car home from the dealership. I have never had such a big-ticket item manifest itself so quickly in my life. I did not have the car in my possession when I started writing this book, yet the car is now in my life even before I complete it!

If there is one reason for the fast manifestation, it is because I focused wholeheartedly on the vibrational essence of my intention (to drive a new luxury car) and let the Universe take care of the rest. Instead of spending my time worrying and fussing over the minor details, I let all those insecurities go. I placed my *complete*, undivided attention on how I would *feel* if I owned a car with all the high-tech features I wanted. How would I feel when driving a smooth, quiet, and spacious car with all the latest gadgets? What would that feel like for me? What is the vibrational essence of what I want? These were the questions that I asked myself repeatedly over the past six months.

Each time I asked myself these questions, I would connect to the vibrational essence of my final physical manifestation. I gave up any attachments to the outcome, such as the dealership I would buy it from or the specific car make or model that I would eventually get. I knew that everything would sort itself out if I held a corresponding vibrational essence on the inside. In other words, the Universe would take care of everything, right down to the smallest details. Whatever that happens in my outer reality would be just right for me.

One final amazing thing happened as a result of letting the Universe lead me in this manner. I ended up buying a car that I would not have "logically" chosen had I gone through a proper comparison process. The car that I eventually bought was not my first choice in my shortlist, because it did not seem to have a number of features that I was looking for. Those features would have been found in another more expensive model.

But that's only part of the story. After buying the car, driving it home, and reading the manual, I realized to my astonishment that it *did* have all the extra add-ons I was looking for; it's just that the dealer had not emphasized them in the marketing material! To make the long story short, this car actually checked all of my boxes while saving me a considerable sum of money. Talk about the Universe leading you and always giving you the full vibrational essence of what you ask for! These techniques can work in your life too, no matter what your current circumstances may be.

Chapter Nine
Practical Ways To Let The Universe Lead You

The subject of receiving divine guidance has fascinated many throughout the ages. We have all heard stories about how Uncle Bob had a dream one night in which a deceased relative revealed a particular course of action to take. True enough, Uncle Bob's furniture business took off after following that advice and his life changed for the better.

These stories are so prevalent in popular culture that many of us to try ways and means to receive divine guidance. We readily buy in to the latest hype or pay huge amounts of money to learn methods that claim to let us access some form of divine database, through which we can learn what our destiny in life is.

Why do you think so many people are clamoring to learn about their destiny? Why do you think so many people are desperate to learn what their future holds? I frequently observe the New Age aisle of bookstores filled with readers poring over books on fortune-telling, the oracle, and divination.

Over the years, I realize that many of us have developed an unconscious fear of the future. This deep-seated fear arises when we do not know what is in store for us and hence the need to use various metaphysical methods to reduce these uncertainties. Ironically, this fear of uncertainty arises due to a lack of understanding about how our Universe operates. When we open our eyes to the benevolent and supportive nature of our Universe by realizing these spiritual principles for ourselves, all our fears and uncertainties instantly fall away. In their place will be a deep feeling of peace and assurance. This is the peace that surpasses all understanding.

Let's first start with the premise that the Universe supports us in all our endeavors. We have already established that the Universe responds instantly to any intention or desire we hold in our consciousness. The moment we hold an intention in our mind, Universal forces act on it immediately by reorganizing energetic forces to support that desire. You feel this in the form of energetic impulses and emotions when you think about your intentions. Notice how good you felt when you connected with the pure essence of joy in your final manifestations. There was nothing else you had to do. All you did was to simply hold that intention singularly in your mind and connect to the underlying aspects of the intention that brought you the greatest joy. This was to assist you in connecting to the pure vibrational essence of your desires. In turn, the Universe responded in an instant by supporting you in feeling that joy.

If you accept this premise that the Universe *always* answers whenever you hold an intention in mind, then it becomes easier to understand the next two points. First, you will realize that no intermediaries or mediums are necessary for the process to take place. You have an always-on, instant connection to the Universe. You do not have to do it through any spiritual guru or psychic although some people may still choose to, since their resistant thoughts and feelings do not allow them to clearly interpret all communications from the Universe. But know that such intermediaries are *always* optional, because we are always receiving divine guidance in the form of inner nudges and impulses.

Second, you start to realize how this uncertainty, which you have always feared and sought to eliminate your entire life, actually represents *your greatest freedom in life!* Let me repeat this again because it is such an important point: The uncertainty that we seek to eliminate from our lives actually represents our greatest freedom. It is a testament to our abilities to create absolutely anything we want as powerful creators with no limits. If this ability to create did not exist, there would be no "uncertainty" about the future as there would only be a single fatalistic path that we could take. The uncertainty actually means that can choose to create anything we want.

So when people seek to eliminate the "uncertainty" from their lives, what they are really hoping to do is to remove their feelings of fear and worry about the future. They certainly do not wish to remove their own abilities to choose and create as powerful creators! Thus, know that when you say you want to feel "secure" about the future, what you are actually referring to is the absence of fear as opposed to the absence of choices.

Now let's get to the million-dollar question: How does one receive divine guidance from the Universe on what to do next? What are the steps that we have to do to start the process? I hope the answer is already obvious to you by now: One does not "choose" to receive divine guidance. One is already receiving it *all the time* whether he likes it or not. We can only choose whether to turn our backs on the guidance received or to act on it.

When I say that the Universe always supports us in all of our endeavors and leads us towards our greater good, I do not mean using the Universe as a divination tool. Far too many people misinterpret these spiritual teachings to mean that the Universe will chart a clear path for them and tell them exactly what to do in a step-by-step manner. The mistake these people make is in hoping that the Universe will *decide* what they want for them. The Universe can never decide on your behalf because doing so will mean denying your own abilities as a powerful creator.

There was a period in my life where not much outer progress happened over a few years. Those were the most stagnant years of my life and I was driven to the edge of depression. I had totally lost all drive to create, stopped asking for the things I wanted, and fallen into a general state of apathy. Looking back, I realize it is because I had misinterpreted these

Universal principles. I had read that the Universe always leads us to our greater good, and hence I spent most of my day sitting there and just waiting for divine signs. I refused to do anything until I identified something that looked remotely like a divine signal. I became superstitious and read into everything without even realizing it. Unbeknownst to me, what I was asking for was not divine guidance but for the Universe to *decide and live on my behalf*! I was desperately telling the Universe to *choose* my future path and take responsibility for my life, something that it could not do!

If things appear stagnant in your life at the moment, the first thing to ask is if you are sitting around and waiting for some higher being to make a particular choice for you. Are you expecting the Universe to lead your life for you? We often do so without realizing it to absolve ourselves from making wrong or supposedly bad decisions. But know that you have to make the first move. You have to choose and hold your intention first before the Universe can support you in any of your endeavors.

The good news is that once you make the first move and decide on what you want, Universal forces immediately conspire to make your desires happen, no matter what you have chosen for yourself. All I had to do was to hold a very light intention for my new car, connect with the vibrational essence of it, and let the Universe take care of the rest. If I had said or thought "Universe, decide on the mode of transportation I need" without even specifying that

I was looking for a car, I doubt the manifestation would have taken place at all!

How you feel on the inside (your inner state) gives you a clue as to how your future manifestations will unfold. When I was in a state of apathy, my inner state was filled with feelings of discouragement and various fears about my future. Since the Universe always supports you in your endeavors, my outer reality could only match my inner state, which resulted in *more* stagnation and dead-ends on the outside. Ironically, I received *exactly* what I had asked for, since the vibrational essence of my "desires" was one of apathy and stagnation! The beautiful thing about these Universal Laws is that they work for us in both ways. When you realize this, you realize how much freedom you have as a creator. You have so much freedom that you can choose to suffer, if you wanted to.

Another consequence of awakening to your full potential as a powerful creator is that you don't have to worry about making the wrong choices or bad decisions in life. You know that no matter which path you choose or however outer reality appears to be at the moment, it can always be changed to something better. That's why you never have to worry about whether you are making the best possible choice for yourself in any given moment. Just choose the path that feels best for you right now and you can adjust accordingly as life unfolds. I have found that worrying over whether we are making the "best possible" decision places unnecessary strain and expectations on ourselves. We often do not have the full Universal perspective of the situation, so expecting ourselves to act as if we know the future is unreasonable. I just make the best possible choice (the emotional path with the least resistance) in any moment and let life take care of itself. As a result, things always get straightened out in the end for me.

Chapter Ten
The Reverse Manifestations Process

The intention for each of my books is to provide practical steps that my readers can easily and readily apply to their lives. As we wrap up this book, I would like to offer an overview of the reverse manifestations process. This is the way that I bring myself through the process nowadays, tying in the spiritual principles that we discussed in various parts of this book. Take this overview as more of a prescriptive guide rather than an authoritative set of rules to be followed. As always, allow yourself to be open to all possibilities and let everything that unfolds be all right for you!

The first step to invoking the reverse manifestations process is to decide on what you want. It is all right if you do not know the full specifics of what you want. For example, I did not know the exact car make and model that I wanted. I did not know the exact color that I wanted. But I was very clear on the features that I wanted in my new car and how it would feel like for me when I drove it. You do not need to have complete information when invoking the reverse manifestations process, so don't let that be a stumbling block for you. Far too many people say, "I cannot visualize my desires because I do not know how it looks like!" They then wait for the Universe to "show them" what their desires should look like in full view. Doing so would be making the mistake of asking the Universe to decide on your behalf. Remember that the Universe *can never* lead your life for you.

It is all right to know what you want without knowing all the minor details and specifics. All you need is to connect with the *feeling* of your final manifestation. Suppose that you are looking for a new house without knowing what kind of house it will be or even which neighborhood it will be located in. All of these specifics do not matter. What matters is that you take the time to connect with the *feelings* that you get when you finally own and live in that house. How does that feel like? What is the vibrational essence of that new house? This is taking broad approach to manifestations. Know that when you take a broad and general approach, you take care of your underlying energetic feelings and let the Universe fill in the rest. After all, aren't we all after the feelings behind our physical manifestations? We ask for things because of the positive feelings of joy, security, and peace that they bring us.

Once you have decided on what you want and identified the vibrational essence of it, the next step is to connect with this vibrational essence for three times each day. I recommend that you consciously set aside 5 to 10 minutes each time you do so. Get yourself into an uninterrupted spot where you can close your eyes and just immerse yourself in the vibrational essence of what you ask for. Remember that in trying out this mental exercise, we are not feeling "as if." Neither are we thinking about our intentions and desires as a whole on a very superficial level. Therefore, there is no need to repeat any affirmations or phrases as you engage in this process. There is no need to keep repeating, "I would like a penthouse on Fifth Avenue overlooking the park with 10 bedrooms and a walk-in wardrobe." Instead, connect with the *vibrational essence* of that desire. This is key. How does this penthouse on Fifth Avenue feel like for you? Better still, how does it feel like for you when you finally live in it? Which aspects of the penthouse pleases you the most when you think about it?

If you take the time to connect with the pure essence of joy within your final manifestations, you may be surprised to find that your sessions have absolutely nothing to do with your supposed manifestations. You may find yourself thinking nothing about the penthouse and instead focusing on just the basic, underlying feelings of joy it brings. This is exactly why the process works so well. The reverse manifestation process is so effective because it places you in the Universal flow by connecting you with the pure *vibrational essence* of your desires with absolutely *no contradictory thoughts.* You are in a state of 100 percent pure allowance. When you allow yourself to be in this state, you stop all resistant energies and thought. You are no longer negatively creating. You no longer unconsciously push your desires away from you with thoughts of worry, attachment, or fear. That is when the manifestations *have to happen* very quickly for you. Another wonderful benefit is that all the *other* things you have asked for start flowing into your life as soon as you give up all forms of resistance.

One important note is that you are not trying to make anything happen when engaging in these daily sessions. Don't turn them into a chore. Trying to "make something happen" means you are exerting effort or strain. All these feelings of "trying" affect your inner state. They detract from the pure inner state that we are trying to achieve with this exercise. Therefore, all you need to do is to connect purely and innocently with those feelings of joy on the inside without tainting your inner state with thoughts/feelings about anything else. Just do the exercise purely because it makes you feel so good! I feel so energized after connecting with the pure vibrational essence of my desires that I am ready to take on anything that comes. It feels even better than taking a nap for me. I do it regularly because it feels so good for me!

During the rest of your waking hours, gently observe and notice whether there are any paths of least resistance that present themselves to you with regard to your intentions. The path of least resistance is the easiest path that you are called to take.

Let The Universe Lead You!

You feel inspired to take a particular action because there is something nudging you on the inside to do it, not because you are feeling fearful of the consequences of not doing it. Anytime you feel the need to take a particular course of action, ask yourself this question: Am I taking this action out of love and inspiration, or out of fear and lack? Drop any feelings of fear or lack the moment they arise and let the need to take any fear-based action go. Only act when you feel inspired on the inside.

Divine action always feels like an easy "yes" for you. When you are in the Universal flow and acting on your divine impulses, you do not experience that nagging sense of emotional discord within. You do not second-guess yourself each step along the way. Sure, your logical mind may protest once in a while and you may hear that critical voice in your head talking back to you, telling you how illogical this action seems...but there is also a very deep *inner knowing* that you are on the right path. Try this out for yourself. You'll feel a sense of *deep inner knowing* that confirms you are on the right path even if external evidence appears to the contrary. That is when you know you are acting on the path of least resistance.

The path of least resistance should feel like the path of *no* resistance for you. Each step you take springs from an inner knowing, a clear sense of inspiration with no underlying feelings of fear or worry. If the path of no resistance presents itself for you, take it! You will be so drawn to taking that path that you will not be able to resist or hold yourself back anyway. This is the sheer creative power of these Universal forces. When a couple is so deeply in love, they cannot help but make love with each other. This sense of untethered Universal calling is what we are going for here. Take the smallest possible action that you feel absolutely compelled to… but till then, don't take any action!

Your logical mind may resist the action that you are called to take especially in the beginning. It may come up with various logical objections as to why you should not be taking a particular course of action. When this happens, there is an easy way to deal with these objections. Just ask yourself the previous question again: Am I taking this action out of inspiration and love, or out of fear? If the answer is the former, then by all means take that action! You can never go wrong when you are following your bliss by taking inspired action. There has never been a single instance where someone took an inspired action that led them to something bad. Not a single time. On the other hand, we hear so many stories about how people have acted on inspiration and have come into contact with wonderful fortunes.

The key is to be honest with yourself when answering the question above. Whenever I meet an individual who tells me, "I followed my hunch and it led to an undesirable outcome," I always tell them to closely examine their reasons for acting. Invariably, they will always find that they acted out of fear and somehow convinced themselves that they were acting from inspiration. This has been the case for myself several times in the past. I *thought* I was acting from inspiration, when in fact my strong impulse to take a particular action was actually to avoid a future loss. Any action taken from a position of fear can never lead to desired consequences down the road.

If no paths of least resistance present themselves to you in the moment, fret not. You are also on the right track! This means that you have done everything you could and that there is nothing else for you to do. Sit back, relax, and let the Universe handle the rest of the details! Go about your daily life in a carefree manner knowing that you are living in the Universal flow! Go out and have a good time. Spend a day at the beach or at the theme park. For me, I like to spend a quiet afternoon in the library just reading anything I like. You can take the Universe at its word when it tells you that there is nothing more you have to do. If at any point the situation evolves and some physical action is required on your part, it will be made known to you.

There are two general kinds of manifestations in your life. The first kind will be truly spontaneous manifestations where you do not have to take any physical action to have something come true in your life. For example, you may receive an inheritance, win a lucky draw, receive a gift, or literally find something you want while walking down the pavement. I have found that these happen sometimes and their frequency increases once we open ourselves up to receiving greater good in our lives.

The second kind will be manifestations involving some small step on our part. These manifestations require us to take some form of small inspired action to bring whatever we want into our lives. For example, we may receive an impulse to go take a look at a particular car, read a book, or take a certain course of action. This type of manifestations is more common.

The key is to stop expecting our manifestations to take one form or the other. Give up any expectations and the attachment to their outcome. There are some who dictate that their manifestations be of the first kind only, where they literally "do nothing" to have whatever they want come to them. They may intend, "I want to have money without lifting a finger!" Doing so will be imposing unnecessary constraints on yourself. Oftentimes, the resulting actions you have to take are so small and minuscule that they can hardly be called work! So always be open to the various ways and means through which things you ask for can come into your life.

If you follow the steps described above, you'll find your life changing for the better in two big ways. The first major improvement will be receiving the things that you are currently asking for. You will find things happening so quickly the moment you ask for them that you no longer walk around in a state of lack and wanting. Whenever a new desire is born within you, the means to fulfill that desire will also be simultaneously known to you. The manifestation process then unfolds with minimal fuss. You'll live in a rewarding cycle of asking and receiving with very little time lag or negative feelings in between. This is the state of highest empowerment and creativity, knowing that you have the power to create anything you want in life.

The second improvement is that long-standing desires from the past will start to come true for you as well. This is a natural consequence of doing the inner work and letting go of any unconscious resistance that you have picked up along the way. The Universe does not discern between "this" desire and "that" desire. It groups everything you want according to their vibrational (energetic) essence. Therefore, when you follow the steps in this book and get yourself to that vibrational place first...that is when *all the things* that match those good feelings start appearing in your life.

All the good—and more—flows into your life when you decide what you want, let go, and let the Universe lead you! Take heed of its guidance!

About The Author

Richard Dotts is a modern-day spiritual explorer. An avid student of ancient and modern spiritual practices, Richard shares how to apply these timeless principles in our daily lives. For more than a decade, he has experimented with these techniques himself, studying why they work and separating the science from the superstition. In the process, he has created successful careers as an entrepreneur, business owner, author and teacher.

Leading a spiritual life does not mean walking away from your current life and giving up everything you have. The core of his teachings is that you can lead a spiritual and magical life starting right now, from where you are, in whatever field you are in.

You can make a unique contribution to the world, because you are blessed with the abilities of a true creator. By learning how to shape the energy around you, your life can change in an instant, if you allow it to!

Richard is the author of more than 20 bestsellers on the science of manifestation and reality creation.

An Introduction to the Manifestations Approach of Richard Dotts

Even after writing more than 20 bestsellers on the subject of creative manifestations and leading a fulfilling life, Richard Dotts considers himself to be more of an adventurous spiritual explorer than a spiritual teacher or "master", as some of his readers have called him by.

"When you apply these spiritual principles in your own life, you will realize that everyone is a master, with no exceptions. Everyone has the power to design and create his own life on his own terms," says Richard.

"Therefore, there is no need to give up your power by going through an intermediary or any spiritual medium. Each time you buy into the belief that your good can only come through a certain teacher or a certain channel…you give up the precious opportunity to realize your own good. My best teachers were those who helped me recognize the innate power within myself, and kept the faith for me even when I could not see this spiritual truth for myself."

Due to his over-questioning and skeptical nature (unaided by the education which he received over the years), Richard struggled with the application of these spiritual principles in his early years.

After reading thousands of books on related subjects and learning about hundreds of different spiritual traditions with little success, Richard realized there was still one place left unexplored.

It was a place that he was the most afraid to look at: **his inner state.**

Richard realized that while he had been applying these Universal principles and techniques dutifully on the outside, his inner state remained tumultuous the whole time. Despite being well-versed in these spiritual principles, he was constantly plagued with negative feelings of worry, fear, disappointment, blame, resentment and guilt on the inside during his waking hours. These negative feelings and thoughts drained him of much of his energy and well-being.

It occurred to him that unless he was free from these negative feelings and habitual patterns of thought, any outer techniques he tried would not work. That was when he achieved his first spiritual breakthrough and saw improvements in his outer reality.

Taking A Light Touch
The crux of Richard's teachings is that one has to do the inner work first by tending to our own inner

states. No one else, not even a powerful spiritual master, can do this for us. Once we have restored our inner state to a place of *zero*, a place of profound calmness and peace…that is when miracles can happen. Any subsequent intention that is held with <u>a light touch</u> in our inner consciousness quickly becomes manifest in our outer reality.

Through his books and teachings, Richard continually emphasizes the importance of taking a light touch. This means adopting a carefree, playful and detached attitude when working with these Universal Laws.

"Whenever we become forceful or desperate in asking for what we want, we invariably delay or withhold our own good. This is because we start to feel even more negative feelings of desperation and worry, which cloud our inner states further and prevent us from receiving what we truly want."

To share these realizations with others, Richard has written a series of books on various aspects of these manifestation principles and Universal Laws. Each of his books touches on a different piece of the manifestation puzzle that he has struggled with in the past.

For example, there are certain books that guide readers through the letting-go of negative feelings and the dropping of negative beliefs. There are books that talk about how to deal with self-doubt and a lack of faith in the application of these spiritual principles. Yet other books offer specific techniques for holding focused intentions in our inner consciousness. A couple of books deal with advanced topics such as nonverbal protocols for the manifestation process.

Richard's main goal is to break down the mysterious and vast subject of spiritual manifestations into easy to understand pieces for the modern reader. While he did not invent these Universal Laws and is certainly not the first to write about them, Richard's insights are valuable in showing readers how to easily apply these spiritual principles despite leading modern and hectic lifestyles. Thus, a busy mother of three or the CEO of a large corporation can just as easily access these timeless spiritual truths through Richard's works, as an ancient ascetic who lived quietly by himself.

It is Richard's intention to show readers that miracles are still possible in our modern world. When you experience the transformational power of these teachings for yourself, you stop seeing them as unexpected miracles and start seeing them as part of your everyday reality.

Do I have to read every book in order to create my own manifestation miracles?
Because Richard is unbounded by any spiritual or religious tradition, his work is continuously evolving based on a fine-tuning of his own personal experiences. He does, however, draw his inspiration from a broad range of teachings. Richard writes for the primary purpose of sharing his own realizations and not for any commercial interest, which is why he has

shied away from the publicity that typically comes with being a bestselling author.

All of his books have achieved bestseller status with no marketing efforts or publicity, a testament to the effectiveness of his methods. An affiliation with a publishing house could mean a pressure to write books on certain popular subjects, or a need to censor the more esoteric and non-traditional aspects of his writing. Therefore, Richard has taken great steps to ensure his freedom as a writer. It is this freedom that keeps him prolific.

One of Richard's aims is to help readers apply these principles in their lives with minimal struggle or strain, which is why he has offered in-depth guidance on many related subjects. Richard himself has maintained that there is no need to read each and every single one of his books. Instead, one should just narrow in to the particular aspects that they are struggling with.

As he explains in his own words, "You can read just one book and completely change your life on the basis of that book if you internalized its teachings. You can do this not only with my books, but also with the books of any other author."

"For me, the journey took a little longer. One book could not do it for me. I struggled to overcome years of negative programming and critical self-talk, so much so that reading thousands of books did not help me as well. But after I reached that critical tipping point, when I finally 'got it', then I started to get everything. The first book, the tenth book, the hundredth book I read all started to make sense. I could pick up any book I read in the past and intuitively understand the spiritual essence of what the author was saying. But till I reached that point of understand within myself, I could not do so."

Therefore, one only needs to read as many books as necessary to achieve a true understanding on the inside. Beyond that, any reading is for one's personal enjoyment and for a fine-tuning of the process.

Which book should I start with?
There is no prescribed reading order. Start with the book that most appeals to you or the one that you feel most inspired to read. Each Richard Dotts book is self-contained and is written such that the reader can instantly benefit from the teachings within, no matter which stage of life they are at. If any prerequisite or background knowledge is needed, Richard will suggest additional resources within the text.

Other Books by Richard Dotts

Many of these titles are progressively offered in various formats (both in hard copy and eBook formats). Our intention is to eventually make all these titles available in hard copy format.

- **Banned Manifestation Secrets**
  It all starts here! In this book, Richard lays out the fundamental principles of spiritual manifestations and explains common misconceptions about the "Law of Attraction." This is also the book where Richard first talks about the importance of one's inner state in creating outer manifestations.

- **Come and Sit With Me (Book 1): How to Desire Nothing and Manifest Everything**
  If you had one afternoon with Richard Dotts, what questions would you ask him about manifesting your desires and the creative process? In Come and Sit With Me, Richard candidly answers some of the most pressing questions that have been asked by his readers. Written in a free-flowing and conversational format, Richard addresses some of the most relevant issues related to manifestations and the application of these spiritual principles in our daily lives. Rather than shying away from tough questions

about the manifestation process, Richard dives into them head-on and shows the readers practical ways in which they can use to avoid common manifestation pitfalls.

- **The Magic Feeling Which Creates Instant Manifestations**

  Is there really a "magic feeling", an inner state of mind that results in almost instant manifestations? Can someone live in a perpetual state of grace, and have good things and all your deepest desires come true spontaneously without any "effort" on your part? In this book, Richard talks about why the most effective part of visualizations lies in the feelings…and how to get in touch with this magic feeling.

- **Playing In Time And Space: The Miracle of Inspired Manifestations**

  In Playing In Time And Space, Richard Dotts shares the secrets to creating our own physical reality from our current human perspectives. Instead of seeing the physical laws of space and time as restricting us, Richard shares how anyone can transcend these perceived limitations of space and time by changing their thinking, and manifest right from where they are.

- **Allowing Divine Intervention**
  Everyone talks about wanting to live a life of magic and miracles, but what does a miracle really look like? Do miracles only happen to certain spiritual people, or at certain points in our lives (for example, at our most desperate)? Is it possible to lead an everyday life filled with magic, miracles and joy?

  In Allowing Divine Intervention, Richard explains how miracles and divine interventions are not reserved for the select few, but can instead be experienced by anyone willing to change their current perceptions of reality.

- **It is Done! The Final Step To Instant Manifestations**
  The first time Richard Dotts learnt about the significance of the word "Amen" frequently used in prayers…goosebumps welled up all over his body and everything clicked in place for him. Suddenly, everything he had learnt up to that point about manifestations made complete sense.

  In It Is Done!, Richard Dotts explores the hidden significance behind these three simple words in the English language. Three words, when strung together and used in the right fashion, holds the keys to amazingly accurate and speedy manifestations.

- **Banned Money Secrets**
  In Banned Money Secrets of the Hidden Rich, Richard explains how there is a group of individuals in our midst, coming from almost every

walk of life, who have developed a special relationship with money. These are the individuals for whom money seems to flow easily at will, which has allowed them to live exceedingly creative and fulfilled lives unlimited by money. More surprisingly, Richard discovered that there is not a single common characteristic that unites the "hidden rich" except for their unique ability to focus intently on their desires to the exclusion of everything else. Some of the "hidden rich" are the most successful multi-millionaires and billionaires of our time, making immense contributions in almost every field.

Richard teaches using his own life examples that the only true, lasting source of abundance comes from behaving like one of the hidden rich, and from developing an extremely conducive inner state that allows financial abundance to easily flow into your life.

- **The 95-5 Code: for Activating the Law of Attraction**
Most books and courses on the Law of Attraction teach various outer-directed techniques one can use to manifest their desires. All is well and good, but an important question remains unanswered: What do you do during the remainder of your time when you are not actively using these manifestation techniques? How do you live? What do you do with the 95% of your day, the majority of your waking hours when you are not actively

asking for what you want? Is the "rest of your day" important to the manifestation process?

It turns out that what you do during the 95% of your time, the time NOT spent visualizing or affirming, makes all of the difference.

In The 95-5 Code for activating the Law of Attraction, Richard Dotts explains why the way you act (and feel) during the majority of your waking hours makes all the difference to your manifestation end results.

- **Inner Confirmation for Outer Manifestations**

How do you know if things are on their way after you have asked for them?

What should you do after using a particular manifestation technique?

What does evidence of your impending manifestations feel like?

You may not have seen yourself as a particularly spiritual or intuitive person, much less an energy reader…but join Richard Dotts as he explains in Inner Confirmation for Outer Manifestations how everyone can easily perceive the energy fields around them.

- **Mastering the Manifestation Paradox**

The Manifestation Paradox is an inner riddle that quickly becomes apparent to anyone who has been exposed to modern day Law of Attraction and manifestation teachings. It is an inner state that seems to be contradictory to the person practicing it, yet one that is associated with inevitably fast physical manifestations—that of *wanting* something and yet at the same time *not wanting* it.

Richard Dotts explains why the speed and timing of our manifestations depends largely on our mastery of the Manifestation Paradox. Through achieving a deeper understanding of this paradox, we can consciously and deliberately move all our desires (even those we have been struggling with) to a "sweet spot" where physical manifestations *have to occur* very quickly for us instead of having our manifestations happen "by default."

- **Today I Am Free: Manifesting Through Deep Inner Changes**

In Today I Am Free, Richard Dotts returns with yet another illuminating discussion of these timeless Universal Laws and spiritual manifestation principles. While his previous works focused on letting go of the worry and fear feelings that prevent our manifestations from happening in our lives, Today I Am Free focuses on a seldom discussed aspect of our lives that can affect our manifestations in a big way: namely our interaction with others and the judgments, opinions and perceptions that other people may hold of us. Richard Dotts shows readers simple ways in which they can overcome their constant feelings of fear and self-consciousness to be truly free.

- **Dollars Flow To Me Easily**
  Is it possible to read and relax your way into financial abundance? Can dollars flow to you even if you just sat quietly in your favorite armchair and did "nothing"? Is abundance and prosperity really our natural birthright, as claimed by so many spiritual masters and authors throughout the ages?

  Dollars Flow To Me Easily takes an alternative approach to answering these questions. Instead of guiding the reader through a series of exercises to "feel as if" they are already rich, Richard draws on the power of words and our highest intentions to dissolve negative feelings and misconceptions that block us from manifesting greater financial abundance in our lives.

- **Light Touch Manifestations: How To Shape The Energy Field To Attract What You Want**
  Richard covers the entire manifestation sequence in detail, showing exactly how our beliefs and innermost thoughts can lead to concrete, outer manifestations. As part of his approach of taking a light touch, Richard shows readers how to handle each component of the manifestation sequence and tweak it to produce fast, effective manifestations in our daily lives.

- **Infinite Manifestations: The Power of Stopping at Nothing**
  In Infinite Manifestations, Richard shares a practical, step-by-step method for erasing the unconscious memories and blocks that hold our

manifestations back. The Infinite Release technique, "revealed" to Richard by the Universe, is a quick and easy way to let go of any unconscious memories, blocks and resistances that may prevent our highest good from coming to us. When we invoke the Infinite Release process, we are no longer doing it alone. Instead, we step out of the way, letting go and letting God. We let Universal Intelligence decide how our inner resistances and blocks should be dissolved. All we need to do is to intend that we are clear from these blocks that hold us back. Once the Infinite Release process is invoked, it is done!

- **Let The Universe Lead You!**
Imagine what your life would be like if you could simply hold an intention for something…and then be led clearly and precisely, every single time, to the fulfilment of your deepest desires. No more wondering about whether you are on the "right" path or making the "right" moves. No more second-guessing yourself or acting out of desperation—You simply set an intention and allow the Universe to lead you to it effortlessly!

- **Manifestation Pathways: Letting Your Good Be There…When You Get There!**
Imagine having a desire for something and then immediately intuiting (knowing) what the path of least resistance should be for that desire. When you allow the Universe to lead you in this manner and unfold the manifestation pathway of least resistance to you, then life becomes as

effortless as knowing what you want, planting it in your future reality and letting your good be there when you get there…every single time! This book shows you the practical techniques to make it happen in your life.

- **And more…**

LET THE UNIVERSE LEAD YOU!

Made in United States
Troutdale, OR
04/17/2025